Eve Heads Back

Eve Heads Back

Poems by

Joanne Leva

Cover design by Shay Culligan
Cover art by Eric Medlin

ISBN: 978-1-952326-63-9

Kelsay Books
502 South 1040 East, A-119
American Fork, Utah 84003

For David Kime

Acknowledgments

I admire and loved working with the gifted and talented Dr. Christopher Bursk on the concept and development of this book. I owe so much gratitude to the Winter Workshop poets, who meet at Bucks County Community College in Newtown, PA—especially The Stalwart Poets. Thank you for sticking around after break.

And thank you to all of my friends who inspire me: Leonard Gontarek, Chad Frame, Liz Chang, Grant Clauser, Hayden Saunier, Doris Ferleger, Amy Small-McKinney, Sean Webb, Susan Charkes, Tom Mallouk, Helen Mirkil, Cleveland Wall, Ethel Rackin, Margaret Almon, Bernadette McBride, Lynn Levin, Lorraine Henrie Lins, Vasiliki Katsarou, Joe Chelius, Eric Medlin, Cathleen Cohen, Joanne Coppens, Paul Siegell, Ernie Hilbert, Brigette Erwin, Yolanda Wisher, Louisa Schnaithmann, Elise Brand, Steve Pollack, Marilyn Gross, Jim Fillman, Rodger Lowenthall, Joe Tice, Tishon Woolcock, and Eve's guardian angel, David Kime.

But most of all, I want to thank two very important people: my grandsons, Marc Vincent and Dominic John Schoettle, for the way their eyes light up when I enter the room.

I would like to thank the Philadelphia Calligraphers Society for including the poem, "God Walks into a Bar," in *Scripta* (July 2019).

I would also like to thank the following publications for including some of the work found here:

E-Verse Radio: "Eden Imagined and Exotic"

Kelsay Books: "A Journal of True Confessions" (previously appeared in *Eve Would Know,* 2017)

Rag Queen Periodical: "Eve Is an Echo," "Eve Pounds Keys," "Harlot"

Schuylkill Valley Journal: "Overture," "The Daughter Letters," "Eve Is an Echo" (previously published in *Rag Queen Periodical*)

Transcendent Visions: "Apocalypse"

Contents

Section 7 As in the Beginning, So in the End

Section 1
In the Garden

God Walks into a Bar

God walks into a bar
and says, *Let there be light!*

Eve holds her Zippo
lighter in the air

in flickering tribute.
She pierces the darkness.

In the Beginning Was the Word

1

Eve Falls into the Distance

Eve cups her hands
behind her ears

to hear the barely
discernable hum

of the computer,
then brings herself to life.

2

Eve Eliminates Dead Air

The conversation
Eve has with herself

goes like this:
I care about you

I'm glad you're here
followed by shoulder shrugs and hiccups.

3

Adam Breaks the Ice

His body language shows
he is excited
Eve is in the room.

He wonders
what words will propel
her in his direction.

Adam raises his eyebrows
and tips his drink
as if to toast Eve,

then mouths, *Hello.*
Eve utters invitingly,
It's so crowded in here, isn't it?

4

The Importance of Underwear

Eve exudes
a certain confidence

that excites Adam.
Proof there is a heaven.

5

An Old Photo Takes Eve

Eve traces the anatomy
of her spirit animal.

Adam ignites the legend
sitting at a campfire.

Meaning emerges.
The story unfolds

like the aroma that rises
from a pot of stew.

6

Always Ten Steps Ahead

After their first encounter,
Eve wonders

if she'll ever see
Adam again.

She toys
with visions of the future

and analyzes awkward feelings.
There is no need

to be a live wire.
Could he be the one?

Overture

From the throne
of her pen,

Girl writes and writes
about everything that resides

in the dark
convolutions

of her mind.
Her gestures articulate,

Why don't you listen to what I'm not saying?
Adam whispers, faintly,

his appetite
for sensual stimulus

is re-directed
to Land of Girl.

By mid-summer,
nights grow.

By autumn,
the location of Land

of Girl is more defined
in bold outline

like an episodic
strip-cartoon.

The two legendary
characters embody

ideals of visitors
portrayed in colorful robes.

Adam and the curvaceous figure
of Girl crowd the edges

of each squared-off
section of the frame.

Adam remembers himself,
then tells Girl

what he needs.
Girl replies phonetically,

saying she will dwell
in his location

eternally.
He feels she is he

and she feels he is she
and that bodes well.

Eve Asks a Magic 8-Ball a Kick-Ass Question

So what does the squeaky wheel get?

The Way to Eve's Heart Is Through Adam's Toolbox

Adam keeps his temper
with difficult screws.

He doesn't risk
stripping threads

and turning a fairly
simple job

into a hair-puller.
Eve parks a nice even stroke.

But Pretty

Eve awakens
in Adam's bed,

it is late afternoon
and she is still

dressed.
The sheets are rumpled

and the pillow
is damp

with sweat.
Gauzy curtains hang

limp against the open
window. The air

is heavy.
Nevertheless

the yellow room
is full of promise.

When All Else Fails, Eve Sweet Talks Adam

Eve chimes in, *This*
is a selfish move, I know.

Thank you for admitting to that,
Adam pleads.

Yeah, I know, but I need to do
what I need to do.

A Wonderful Beautiful Blank

Eve feels
ephemeral

when she's
weeding

the garden.
She breaks

ground,
calls for corn

and tomatoes
from the loose,

crumbly, sweet-
smelling earth.

Section 2
Interlude: The Garden Still with Us

Ode to Olives

Thick, dark skin, soft and cold-pressed,
supple enough to break

at first bite,
baby brochette!

Open mouth receives the pearl.
Delicious fruit donkey, olive.

Shiny black complexion
magnifies my flower tongue.

Like dissolving sugar. Every gland
arrested, every node

prepared for final collapse.
Cure me in brine!

Eden Imagined and Exotic

Smoke ocean
and buttermilk sky

illuminate the night.
Beacons

swagger
in phantom shade.

Underpopulated earth
of rock and flora

rendered in green-gray;
a paradise teeming

with socially engaged nudes,
and oversized fruit.

Lady 'Godiva
feasts on cherries.

In the high distance,
veiled creatures take flight.

A Sprinkling of Lime

Keen cold viridian.
Origin of soil.

Rough road map, moss
and green grass cradle.

Impell me, O little difficulty!
Break the fourth wall!

Entangled joker, turnip leaves.
Unworldly, silver streak

and box-office hit.
Ad lib without restriction

naïve block of granite,
you improbable and popular punchline.

Exciting Offer

Dear Eve,

There is only one way to convince you that the Boaz Bath Beads
are the last word in lasting beauty. I am enclosing sample packets
of two of our most popular scents, Gardenia and Lily of the Valley
of the Shadow of Death. Try them and see if you don't notice
a big difference.

The Good Samaritan

Grave Empire

Lizard-like creature
resumes his place

on the grass,
a squirrel

in its jaws.
Rabbit gulfs in meadow.

Siamese cat faces
the dog and sobs.

The skyline matches
the lake behind it.

Ordinary fruit appears engorged.
Figures engage

in amorous activity.
A man sinks his right hand

close to his genitals.
The bare buttocks

of another dimples.
Fish walk on land and birds

dwell in hot water.
Large explosions

in the background
throw blazing light.

Section 3
The Expulsion: Revisited

And Shit Like This

When Adam mentions
there has been

some controversy
about the apple,

Eve coyly responds,
Has there?

New Agey

Eve smiles
when she speaks,

taking
deep breaths

to avoid
squeaky voice syndrome.

She only appears
sure of herself.

Eve's American Dream

—Critical Edition

Eve Delivers the First Dramatic Speech of Her Career

A hush falls
over the Garden.

"God Bless America"
plays on a scratchy

gramophone.
The curtain rises

on a lit stage.
The audience

leans in
to listen

as a statuesque
part myth part

modern woman
steps forward.

Dear Lord

I feel dreadful about ruining your enchanted world yesterday by eating a quince from the Tree.

You certainly did everything you could to prevent the situation, and I apologize most humbly for ignoring good taste and common sense in pursuing a "discussion" that was completely inappropriate.

I talked to Adam first thing this morning and attempted to mend my fences there, but I feel a great deal worse about what I did to you. The first two hours were delightful.

I hope you will someday be able to forgive me for wrecking the last half-hour.

Eve

Eve Is an Echo

Offers to tell
for the hundredth time
the story of the lazy apple.

Plays the game
of telling and retelling
the tale of the Great Bungle.

Amuses herself
by keeping
an enormous chronicle.

Insists on leaving
the temporary oasis
by walking backwards.

Bonus

Thanks for taking care of the hamsters while we're away, Alice. If you could stop by once a day, that would be great.

Please give everybody one-quarter cup of hamster food and fill their water bottles.

Furball can have an apple slice and Marigold a banana slice from the fruit in the plastic container

(they don't care if it's old and brown). The others don't need any special treats.

We'll be back before the cages need cleaning, so no worries about that.

Adam

Audible Click

Eve writes
to the County
Pathologist.

She solicits
any variant or deviant
information

on the study
of passions and
conditions.

She explains she
is a mystery
looking for a game plan.

Peace of Mind

Dear Eve,

Thank you for your inquiry about Holy Supper Wines. Enclosed are several brochures describing our vineyards and products and a list of vendors in your area.

Sincerely,

The Wise and Foolish Virgins

A Kiss to the Dream

At sunset
Eve sends Adam

a folded note
with a streamer attached

signed,
Mistaken Identity.

Every Whim-Wham

Eve cooks gourmet snails
with a huge roast,

blood pours out
as Adam carves.

Zucchini steams
and heavy pudding

puddles on the plate.
Eve invokes more

insatiable lust
than Adam can bear.

Abel Learns to Say Yes

Eve asks Abel
to swallow a forkful

of broccoli
before she can count

to three. Abel complies.
What a great yes

that was,
she whispers,

then observes something
slowly swallows her.

Adam Changes Props

Adam puts away
fine breakables,

places the CD player
on a high shelf

and installs a lock
on the bathroom door.

Eve Goes Cold Turkey

which is not
the same

thing as actual
happiness.

On Pruning Fruit Trees

Make all wounds clean,
all cuts deep
and close to the bone.

Never leave a stub
when heading back.
Cut above

a healthy bud
pointing
in the desired direction.

Remove overbearing branches
and undercut
until the saw binds,

then press down
until you hear
it snap.

Section 4
Interlude: Meditation on Loss

Fame

It's not how
at twelve-

years-old
and belted

to the backseat
of my father's

convertible,
I saw

"Uncle Jack,"
a toothless man,

yellow with age
on the street,

a brown paper bag,
in the shape

of a starlet,
in his hands.

It's how
at twelve,

my dad
coaxed me

to sit
on Jack's lap

at the VFW
where my grandfather

tended bar.
How he

encouraged him
to kiss me.

Memory

I was about eight years old,
my brother five,
my sister four.

A big, smoking bus
was parked out front
of Lit Brothers,

a long-gone department store,
where my grandmother
worked Sunday afternoons.

On this particular
traumatic Sunday
(our monthly paternal visit)

our father led us
onto the bus,
which was a kind

of Fun House
for cops and such–
an electric chair

on full display
with worn leather
wrist straps,

and extra large
bronze buckles,
with an eerie

little metal cap
attached to the top
that reminded me

of my mother's
spaghetti strainer
at home.

Be a good girl,
my dad said,
pointing to the chair,

or they'll put you
in one of these
and fry you like an egg.

Dead Windows

...and then you left, as you were to leave over and over...
—Sharon Olds, "Monarchs"

I struggled

    to feel you

as you left

I listened

    to muddled talk

in the hallway

I looked into lifeless

    pale blue portholes

Not a bad death

Even now as I relive

    your passing

I remember

your cheeks

    How they released their pain

Revival

When there appeared
to be no life at all,

when nothing moved,
nothing flew

overhead.
The thirsty dead

fell silent
as two white lines

in the middle of the road.
Soft-spoken

and slight, her long
flinty hair

a brittle box of bone.
She mourned

like someone who lost
possession

of her entire self,
every mile

a swell.
But earth

held its peace
under her thunder

and the lightening
that dictated rain.

Then the simple
water trickles

onto ceramic dunes.
Condensation forms.

Rebirth emerges
in the eighth hour

and another storm
ensues,

followed by the flowering
of newly wet earth.

Water pools and glistens again.
In the marshes,

thickets of reeds
amid a torrent of water

run across moist hills
and lap against her toes.

Her natural body
urgent to live

the whole damn story
by the Great River.

On Dying

I die millions of times
each day, in countless ways.

It's only the gradation of pain I notice.
My toast burns. I cease.

There is no more cream. I'm gone.
Never to return the same

when my daughter throws me from her arms. I go
through a traffic light. I give up.

I work late.
I depart.

My desire fades.
I leave.

My life is a half-open book,
a novel of peculiar imperfections.

But death brings me
to life, so I smile

in the face of it.
Sigh

with the thought of doing it
again'and again.

Personally, I Ad

DWF
Divorced White Female
in search of
ISO
AWM
Average White Male
with no disease
WND.
Someone who likes
SWL
boating
pizza
movies
theater
and spontaneity,
BPMT and S
T and A
S and M.
OK maybe
a thumb sucker
someone to go boating with
someone
to eat pizza with
someone
to lay me down
like a rug
on the basement floor.
ISO
a man
WND
if you please.
Amen
if you please me.

Extraordinary Kindness

As I dance
among your long
and leafy limbs,
I am happy.

As I rest
beneath your sheer
and speckled shade,
I lack nothing.

As I ripen
from your sweet
and tender tow,
I have hope.

Section 5
Cain and Abel: A Home Movie

Eve Practices with Play Phones

Eve can't twist
her neck to glimpse

Cain in the dining room.
This is how mommy talks

on the phone,
she calls.

He doesn't answer.
She chatters on,

And this is how Cain plays
while mommy is on the phone.

He comes crawling,
tries to climb her,

but keeps slipping back.

One-Man Show

Cain blows food
from his mouth

as quick as Adam
can shovel it in.

Cain seems to enjoy
the splash it makes

as it consecrates the floor.

Supernatural Parenting

Adam tries hard
not to squelch
Cain's exploratory instincts.

Adam knows
Because I say so
can stifle a small child.

Adam Observes the Sabbath

A disappearing box
is the last thing

in the world
Adam wants to make,

but he spends days
in the basement

building that contraption.
Cain loves the latches,

especially the escape hatch.

Eve Pounds Keys

Eve pounds keys
at the typewriter

until a wave of nausea
washes over her.

Young Cain looks
at the pounding

with fascination
a dozen times a day.

A large ivy-covered
water tower, terraced into

one side of the mountain,
used for rural broadcasting,

is full of static
and unexpected announcements.

Now, Today, Forward

Dear Eve,

I would like to meet with you to discuss Cain's progress this year.

Can you give me 20 minutes sometime next week?

Hope to hear from you soon.

Miss Hall

Interrogation

She said her name
was Eve,
but added
some people call her

Penelope.
She appeared
to be writing
a memoir

she guarded zealously.
She said
she was a teacher
in Eden

before moving to Reno.
She lived there briefly
with a television
producer

and evangelist.
She returned to town
about three weeks
before the incident.

Dreadful News

Dear Eve and Adam,

We felt so bad when we heard about the murder. Something similar happened to us, and it affected me much more deeply and took longer to get over than I would have expected. I hope you are not too undone.

Can we help get things back in order? Give us a call, will you!

Carol and Mike Brady

Zebra Card

The first report
after Abel's death

stated he died
from positional

asphyxiation,
but was soon revised.

Suspect

I enrolled in an art class,
but didn't take it
seriously,

assumed
it would be a walk
in the park.

Failing grades
at midterm
jeopardized

my scholarship status,
so I learned
no matter

what I'm doing,
it's not worth doing
at all.

Confidential, Eve

My friends
would probably say

I'm extremely
persistent.

A lot
of people

may have given
up after

The First Rejection.

Section 6
Interlude: Daughters

A Journal of True Confessions

I feel the earth move
and the sky tumble down

      Especially when we fight about food.

Want some porridge? I asked her.
No, she replied.

There's this diner she likes
that serves scrapple and eggs
on porcelain dishes
and all the waitresses wear badges.

I know how to cook scrapple, I said.

On her bed
we talked about morning foods
like cereal and muffins.
The smell of porridge trailed
up the corridor
wrapping around doorways
and into the room.

      I think cereal is like a breakfast shortcut.

Why won't you eat porridge? I asked her.
Because I'm not a bear, she said.
And I hate cereal.

Well, you're having it.

But I hate it.

It's easy.

It's boring.

It's good for you and you're going to eat it.
       I always feel better when I exert my
       maternal authority, like I'm doing what I
       should, like I'm being a real mom.
       Maybe I should wear a badge?

When the porridge cools
we will eat
until we are full
and that will make me happy.

The clouds pushed away from the sky
and the morning sun trickled in
window shade's filtered shadows
dancing like little wall-silhouettes.

A flash of light.
A puff of smoke.
We remembered the bad dream.

       Sometimes my voice echoes in my head.
       I know I told her not to go into the woods,
       not to go, I said.

Do Not
Take the shortcut through the forest.
I've heard bears live there

or you could get lost.

It was a stormy night.
She woke, yelling, *Mommy, I'm scared!*

      From what I could gather, Martha was this
larger-than-life
     creature who was chasing her and she was
running for her life.

Wasn't it the wolf that said, *What big eyes you have,
but your ears, they're so small.*

Didn't you hear your mother?

I didn't get the muffins, Mom.
You went through the woods.

Yes.

Why.

I don't know. How did you know?

I just knew.

      I always wondered how mothers knew
everything, too.

It was dark.
I was lying alone in my bed.
She burst in
pleading to sleep with me.
I said, *No.*
Sleep in your own bed.

The room was still.
The moon shone through
window shade's filtered shadows
dancing like little wall-silhouettes.

I tucked her back into her own small bed.

When morning came
I woke with fury
to find her next to me
in my bed.

Somebody's been lying in my bed! I cried.

I couldn't sleep, she said.

Our eyes met.
The wind blew the chill of the dream
over us again
and we huddled together.
Want some porridge? I asked.
No, she replied.
I want to go to the diner.

The Pillow

10 am
Moving Day.

You are busy
filling dresser drawers

while I unpack sheets
and make your bed.

I notice you packed
your peach-colored pillow,

the one I bought
for naptime at daycare.

A memoir adorns
the dark,

droopy edges
in patterns of drool.

As you and I move,
we work

on letting go
of different things.

The Daughter Letters

1

Dear Daughter,
You say
you love your life
but you are only 10

—and I am counting
the months that you dwelled
within my belly.

2

Dear Daughter,
I held you
close to my skin
and fed your hungry body.

I listened—
as you gasped for air.
I watched your tiny fingers stroke my hand.

3

Dear Daughter,
I remember
all of it—
but those times have turned to dust

—and as we live
in this clay house
we make more.

4

Dear Daughter,
My wish
is that you know
how far I've come

—and that you know
it took this long.

Section 7
As in the Beginning, So in the End

Harlot

Eve calls on desire
and gets no response.

She senses
her Goddess passing.

Could be the last
of the human race.

Eve is up to her neck
in curses.

Eve Wakes Herself Up

She thinks
of an energizing
color like red,

takes in ten
deep breaths,
visualizes breathing

red,
sends it
throughout her body.

The Damn Story

Eve longs
to tell her story.

She tries to get it down
on paper

for seven years—
maybe closer to ten.

She has a title
and scenes

sketched out,
but the characters

raise eyebrows.
Her diary

full of straightaway
scribbled notes.

Eve Takes the Job

Eve takes the job
not because she aspires

to a career, but she wants to get
as far as she can

from housekeeping.
She does feature

writing for *The Judea Times*
and leads the Doctrine Data-Mapper

Department long distance
from her overgrown garden.

Eve Aches to Get into Radio

The big talk
station in town

offers Eve
an audition

for a midday time slot.
Adam wrestles

with his libido
for days.

For Radio and Pantomime

Eve awakes alarmed
over the whole performance.

That fateful day
precisely placed and dated.

Her hand clutches
the banister.

She remembers leaving
the marriage.

As in the beginning,
so in the end.

Eve Gives Herself an Honest Critique

Eve keeps repeating
the same mistake.

Being comfortable
is not something that comes

naturally to her.
Even seasoned broadcasters

admit to recurring
stage fright.

Ode to Eve

You are an elevator pitch
taken seriously.

You are the compelling contrarian
and counter-intuitive timing.

You are an infomercial
entering a room,

the 20-word delivery
of a thousand atoning scriptures.

Apocalypse

Cinders blown to grass,
they watch from the beach.

The captive apostles set up camp
among glittering ruins.

A series of odd jobs
and random associations follow.

Why Eve Signs Up for a Poetry Workshop

A poem
has its way

of listening
and retaining.

Try to put your finger
on what makes it

so radiant.
A poem knows

her value.
She is not defined

by opinions,
but by the One

who makes her.
She is a glistening

mindful jewel.
Gossip, slander, and idle talk

are strangers
to her lips.

A poem keeps her word
and follows through.

Not known
for laziness,

she works diligently
in the fog of fear.

Mystery Gift

It is the moment
alone

which determines
whether Eve

exists or not.
To submerge

completely.
A lockout.

To consciously
remove

the most essential truth—
Eve is a theater.

A drama that springs
from everyday life.

Eve is the City
of Dreams,

Mother
Goddess,

a current
to the past,

an old fear
that compels the first

and final peril.
And so it goes.

About the Author

Author of the poetry collection, *Eve Would Know* (2017), published by Kelsay Books, Joanne Leva is an advocate for creative writing and community service. She is founder and executive director of the Montgomery County Poet Laureate Program (MCPL) and founder and editor-in-chief of Tekpoet, an online poetry manuscript services company.

Leva's poems appear in *50 Over Fifty* (PS Books), *Apiary, Bucks County Writer, E-Verse Radio, Peace Is a Haiku Song* (The Foundry Books), *Rag Queen Periodical, Schuylkill Valley Journal, The American Poetry Review, Transcendent Visions,* among others.

Her poem, "God Walks into a Bar," was featured in a Philadelphia Calligraphers' Society Poetry Reading & Exhibit and companion publication entitled *Scripta* (July 2019).

Go to
www.joanneleva.com
to learn more.

Kelsay Books

Printed in the USA
CPSIA information can be obtained
at www.ICGtesting.com
LVHW010005100424
776892LV00003B/395

9 781952 326639